IT'S THE CLIMB
II

Jean A Williams

Copyright © 2015 Jean A Williams

totalbodyalive.com

Email at williams1771@att.net

All rights reserved.

ISBN-13: 978-0-9888716-1-8

DEDICATION

I would like to thank my friends for being part of my life. I have an amazing bunch of friends who have stuck with me through thick and thin. I haven't always been the person I am now and couldn't have gotten here without all of you. I love you dearly and thank you from the bottom of my heart for not giving up on me.

I am also dedicating this book to a special person. He pushed me and gave me inspiration to do things I have never done before. I lost Isaac in the process of writing this book, but will continue on with what he helped me start. I will forever be grateful for what his love brought to my life.

Isaac Ware
11 April 1965 to 3 February 2015

CONTENTS

Acknowledgments

Life's Struggles	Pg # 7
Love's Hope	Pg # 23
Living Life	Pg # 47
Where the Spirit Leads You	Pg # 63
Into the Strom	Pg #77

ACKNOWLEDGMENTS

Thank you to all of my friends who inspired me to write these words. It was through you I was moved to thought.

Editor – Lina Culps, Linda Stamps, Rick Williams

Illustrator - My daughter Alexis Williams

Life's Struggles

"It is much easier to sit in the valley than to climb the mountain, but if what you are looking for is on the other side you have to climb the mountain. There will always be valleys to sit in, but that mountain may have a time limit."

In the Dark

In the deepest darkest night I sit
And only a flickering light was lit
I try to find my way through it all
I step and stumble through the hall
Fighting my way down memory lane
Struggling through the tears and pain
But is it so real at all
Did I really stumble
Did I ever fall
I think I was held up in the light
But it was I who put up the fight
I could have just let it be
But I always just wanted it for me
Sometimes we just have to let it go
And it's not always for us to know
For God will see you through
And all your struggling will never do

Break Free

I have been broken
I have been beaten
And I have been chained
But what I have learned
Is that I put all of this on myself
Not saying that I deserved it
But that my way of thinking
Kept me from stopping it
If you let your mind control you
You will be in enchained by many
You will be broken and beaten by many
But when you stand up
When you say "I'm important"
"I have worth"
And be strong in yourself
These things won't happen
A beaten woman stays because she thinks she doesn't deserve better
Not because she likes the pain
A woman is enchained because she doesn't believe in herself
Not because she wants to wear them
Once you know and believe that you control things
Your choices will change
Your mindset will change
And you will be free
If your mind says that you are strong and worthy
Than you will be
And you will turn away what doesn't serve you
Don't try and change others to suit you
Because they never will
Change yourself and be free

"Sometimes we have to take the fork in the road because we are meant to go in a different direction than the one we have been traveling. We don't always know the reason or see the light at the end of the tunnel, but believe me the light is there. You have to step out in faith and believe that you are headed in the direction that God wants you to go in. Life happens. It happens for a reason. Trust that God knows what he is doing even if you don't have a clue."

"Never let anyone stop you, hold you back, or discourage you from living your dreams. Remember they are your dreams, what others think is not important."

"Wherever you are at in your life, it's not too late to make changes, live dreams, be better, be healthier, and be happier. It's only too late when you are not here anymore. As long as you are living and breathing you can change your life. The lies we have been told are "We are too old to change" and the lie we tell ourselves is "We can't change" or "We're not going to change". I'm here to tell you, you can. Once you decide to do something and stick to it, you will. Never give up.
The difference between winning and losing is not giving up. Just ask Thomas Edison. I bet he didn't know that he would be just as famous for not giving up as he is for the light bulb."

"Peace lies within. Peace isn't something that someone else can give you."

"A lot of the times we choose things that aren't really all that important in life to focus on. We choose to be angry about the toothpaste cap being left off or the toilet paper being on the wrong way. We spend an exorbitant amount of time on the small stuff. What would happen if we spent that time on something important? What if we didn't let those little things bother us? How do you think our lives and our relationships would change?"

"You don't have time for regrets……regrets are in the past and you can't do anything about them. Live your life for today because it's all you have. Don't live for tomorrow either, because it may never come. Be happy in the moment. Live each day like it's your last and you will live a full and wonderful life."

"The key to life is putting your best foot forward every day. The problem is that we forget which foot is our best one and just don't put one forward at all."

"There are many windows in life……..some we can see and some we cannot. The windows you can't see are the most important. You have to look inside yourself, because the window to your soul will lead you to many things."

"Laughter Changes Everything"

It is not possible to feel bad when you are laughing.

"Just because you change something you are doing doesn't make what you were doing bad or wrong. It just means you have grown and see things differently. We all have done something and then decided it wasn't the right thing for us to do. Life is a process and you never stop changing. If you don't change you aren't living life the way it was intended."

Will You Fall

The life that we live has its ups and downs
We run from day to day without a thought
Do we have our eyes open or closed
Do we think with our minds or our hearts
Or does greed step in
Do we watch where we are going
Thinking about the consequences of our actions
Do other peoples pain matter
When you look in the mirror
Who do you see
Can you wake up with yourself every day
Do you smile and the person in the mirror smiles back
Or do you carry a heavy feeling in your heart
Is what you are doing making you
Or is it really breaking you
We all have to live with the demons we create
Is it really worth it to create them at all?
Only you can make the path
But if you let the path make you
You will fall
Maybe not right away, but you will fall
So if you wake up and don't like the person you see
Go make the person you are a person of substance
Someone whom you can live with
It's never too late

"In order for positive things to come your way you have to have positive thoughts."

"Change is only possible when you shut off the negative voices in your head."

"Peace is within us. We can't fight for it, buy it or find it in someone else. Once we find that peace it will be with us forever. Life may try to take it from us, but we will always know where to find it when we need it."

"Deep inside of you is a person you didn't know you could be. You have to deal with the cobwebs and get rid of them before that person will come out. We can't be the person we were intended to be if we carry around the baggage of our past."

Goodbye

I woke up today in a place that was unfamiliar
Because where I left was my old life
I struggled through many things
Pain often consumed me
I know what I did was wrong, but I couldn't fight it
It had a hold on me that I cannot describe
Know that my pain and suffering was not what I wanted for me
Somehow it sucked me in
I know I had family and friends who cared about me and loved me
And I'm sorry for the pain you now endure
I didn't mean for you to suffer in my suffering
But I didn't know how to stop it
Everyday my life was a struggle
So I hope you can understand now that I'm gone
That I loved you, my family and my friends
My struggle had nothing to do with you
So please be at peace now knowing that I am
That I don't have to struggle anymore
And know this is not the life I would have chosen,
it is the life I had
So don't cry those tears for me
Let me go now
I now have peace that I was never able to find

In Memory of Hollie

If you walk through life in fear,
you will get things to be afraid of.
If you cry through life you will get
more to cry about.
If you hate you will get more things
around you that you will hate
If you feel defeated you will get more
things to defeat you
So you should…….
Walk fearless
Be happy
Love always
Be positive

Time Isn't the Master

Time is only the master of time
You can't make more of it
There is only so much of it
And it will run out for you
Letting time be your master
Will get you loss of time
Wasted time
And no time
Time will not stand still
Time will master itself with or without you
Time will continue long after you're gone
Time itself will never run out
There will always be time
It's only for time
And time has no master
Time is and will be alone
But what you do with time is up to you
You can waste it
You can throw it away
You can wait for it
But time shouldn't be wasted
Because you will lose things
Time shouldn't be thrown away
Because you can't get it back
Time can never be regained
But it will always remain
Whether you use it
Lose it
Find it
Have it
Want it
Or whatever you do with it
So if you choose to let time master you
Remember that it doesn't care about you
It has its own agenda
So what you do with the time you have
Is what's important
But waiting for it will get you nothing
Because no one knows how much time they have

Love's Hope

Forever

I will love you forever
It's not very hard
You hold the key
The only key to my heart

You are a part of me
That I can't describe
You are inside of me
You make me alive

Your words are like sunshine
Like fireworks and stars
They make my day
Always better by far

I long to be with you
Every step of the way
To be there for you
Come what may

To share every moment
The good and the bad
To be each other's strength
That we don't always have

<u>My Love</u>

I give you my love
Much different from the others
It shouldn't be taken lightly
Or put on a shelf nightly
For as you say it can go away
But if you really knew it
You wouldn't have that to say
I'm not like the others
In some ways I'm sure it's true
But you have to let me do this
It's all I know to do
I can't just tell you
Over and over again
Without you letting me show you
It's all just like pretend
I wish you wouldn't compare me
To the others that have passed your way
For I am only me
Today and everyday
I will not tell you of the possibilities
Or that I'm flawless inside
But what I will tell you
Is my love for you will abide
Abide by the laws
That love has set for me
And if you really want me
You will now set me free

My Love Cont'd

Free from the mirrored memories
Of those no longer around
To be able to love you
I have to have clear ground
I may make mistakes
That I'm sure I will
But if you want me to love you
Then it's time to be still
To still your heart from the past

And let them no longer linger
True love will last
Much longer than you figure
See…. what I have learned
Has all prepared me for now
The path I choose to be on
Beside you is where I'm bound

Love's Embrace

The journey
Though it has been long
Was for love
A love that fills all of me
A love that time cannot erase
I embrace this love
I cherish it and hold it close to my heart
Though time has tried to rip it from me
I will not let it out of my grasp
I will not let it slip away
And though I have struggled
I have never struggled with this love
It is so deeply a part of me
It's in everything I see and do
It's you

Love is Love

Love is love
Though it passes through time
Love is love
You forever will be mine
Love is love
As I close my eyes
And dream of you
In the moonlight
Love is love
To the end of the earth
Love is love
And all it's worth
Love is love
To the moon and back
To the end of time
And never will lack
Love is love
In its purest form
Love is love
My heart it adorns
Love is love
To the depths of the sea
Love is love
And will always be

I'm OK

Tears run down my face today
Please don't worry… I'm ok
I think of you
As I always do
And wonder if you still love me too
The way that I love you
I'm having trouble with my heart
It aches for you
When we are apart
And other things creep into my head
That swells my eyes and makes them red
I tell myself that it's ok
I will get through this one more day
So when you look up in the sky
And see a twinkle it's from my eye
As the moon falls on my tears
A twinkle is what will appear
So all the stars up in the sky
Are from my tears I cannot lie
They watch over you in the dead of night
Hoping you will see them till light
I need that strength that you have inside
To get me through this difficult ride
If only I could hide my eyes
They hold me now I'm mesmerized

Memories

Oh my gallant one
You have ridden off into the sun
I have waited for your return
My heart on fire, forever will it burn

I long for your return to me
So far across the deep blue sea
To hold me in your loving arms
And keep me always away from harm

When I go to that place
In my mind I can't erase
I see you there in memories
Forever mine are these

I reach out my hand to you
But to no avail
For it is only in my heart
And it leaves a trail

I see the memories
And the past with you
But that is all I have
For what am I to do?

My heart hurts
For the millionth time
And crying helps
But it's so sublime

I cry the tears
Of the pain I feel
It tears at me
With no appeal

Never Alone

Lay with me on this bed of roses
And I will pull out all the thorns
I will only leave the petals
For they will never be worn

I will replace them with the love I have
With comfort and a kiss
Till it all goes away again
For they will never be missed

I will hold you in my arms
Now and everyday
I will see us through this place
That only comes out gray

But coming out of it
We will never be the same
I will love you till the end of time
And I will always remain

This will change us now
For it has been told
I will love you forever
And forever we will grow old

I will never let you be alone
Or suffer in anyway
For I will be with you my love
Each and everyday

Forever Changed

The winds of time may come and go,
But the winds of love only come once
I'm not talking about average love
But true love
The kind of love you can't describe to anyone
The kind of love that even when you think about it
You can't tell someone else just how much it is
Others won't understand it
And may tell you that it's not right
But only you know the reasons why
And only you understand it
You understand that person better than anyone
That person will have hung your moon and stars
And no matter what
That love will never go away
It is the only love you will ever find that will complete you
That will make you do things
That even you didn't think you could do
It will have you climbing mountains
And crossing raging rivers
That person is the person
You would go to the end of the earth to be with
And only when you are with that person are you truly whole
Most never find this love and some will let it go
Can people live without true love
Yes they can, and most do
But if you find it
It will change you forever
And know that you don't ever want to live without it

"Couple's don't hold hands when they grow old
unless they held hands when they fell in love."

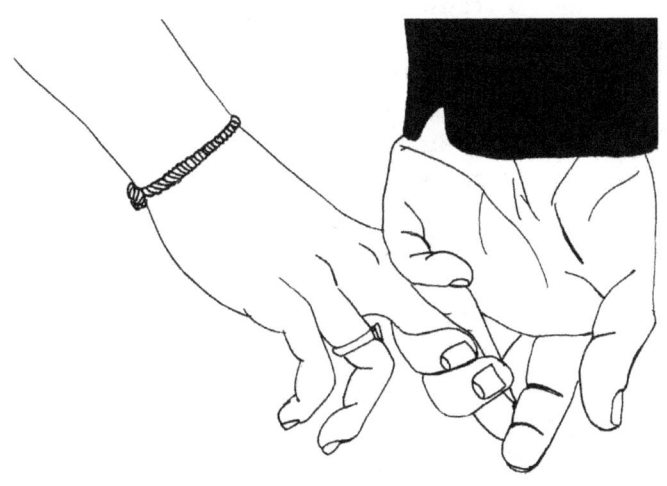

The journey is much better when you can do it all by yourself, but don't have to.

The Stairs Can't Hold Me

Through the stairs
On a misty night
I climb and climb
Without a light
It's like I don't know where I'm going
But I do.....
The stairs have led me right to you
I have stumbled
I have fallen
But I got up again
Because through the door
Is where I was headed
And I'm not giving in

I'm not letting go
I'm not letting them win
For the stairs want to hold me
But again....
I'm not giving in

I climb each step
As if it where for my life
And I know now I will be alright
The door is now open
And I'm going through
Ready to start my life
All over with you

"Do you love someone so much that when you are apart it hurts? Try loving them that much when you are together."

"When you have a mutual love with someone, don't let the little things tear you apart. You can't go through a relationship with your eyes closed. Be present and alive in that relationship, it will not sustain itself. Don't wait until the bliss is gone to revitalize it, that should be done every day. Remember if you do something to take love out you have to do something to put it back in."

"Never underestimate the power of love. Love can conquer all things if you don't let the outside world in."

"Love the one you love like they want to be loved, not how you want to be loved. Take the time to ask. No matter how your relationship is to you, it may not be to the other person. Often times we think we are thinking of the other person, but a lot of the time we are just thinking about ourselves."

"If I had known that loving you was going to be so hard, I would have done it an anyway."

"Sometimes it's only about LOVE, nothing else."

"True love is the most intense feeling you will ever feel. If it goes away over time it wasn't true love. True love transcends time."

"Love with all you have.....no matter how many times."

"Loving someone takes effort. You can't just love and expect everything to just workout. Both people have to want to love each another no matter what."

My dreams were shattered when you left,
Then I realized I can have all my dreams
You just will not be here to share them with me
But I know you're with me each and everyday
And because of you I have more strength to see them though.

"Your love for someone can only be defined by you. Don't let others tell you how that love should be. But in order for you to make the right decisions you have to be whole yourself."

Into My Heart

These are the windows
Into my heart
Look very closely
We're never apart

Waiting for you to open it up
It's where you reside
It's where my love goes
When it's held inside

So many things
You can unfold
I will keep it safe
And never grow old

Until that day
You open it up
And take me away
And fill me up

The beauty it holds
Is for only you
Because no one else
Will ever do

So look deep
Within your heart
And you will see
You have the same part

The missing piece
That goes with mine
To connect the puzzle
Will be divine

Take my hand
And dream a dream
So far out there
It will only seem
To be out of reach
But you will never know
So take my hand
And just let go

Sand

As I sit here on the beach
And the tide washes past
I can't help but think of you
Mesmerized by it fast

As I write I love you
Into the sand
The water washes it away
It's out of my hands

It washes the sand
From beneath my toes
And covers them up
So no one knows

As the sand washes
The writings that I wrote
It takes it away from me
And leaves no hope

But I know in my heart
What the sand doesn't know
And even though it fades
Never will you go

For the sands of time
May come and go
But in my heart
You're already though

You will always have a place
The sand can never erase
And hold it you will
Till I see your face

For my heart isn't like the sand
That changes with the tide
But forever it's in engrained
Forever in my mind

Love Anyway

Loving isn't about letting go
Because we always have memories
Loving isn't about forgetting
Because that isn't possible
One of the greatest things we do in life is to love and be loved
But it is also one of the hardest
Because we will lose many loved ones in our life
And it will be very painful
Sometimes so painful we don't know how we will
Or how we did get through it
I often wonder why we have to go through this cruel process
Why it has to hurt so much
But do we stop loving
No
We love anyway
As in life, death should be a celebration
Not for what we are losing
But for what we had with that person
No regrets
It reminds us that we should always do the right things
Love and be loved
But for ourselves
Live life to the fullest
Don't hold back

A Wish

I wish that I could wake up one day
And my love will have come my way
To stop this never ending stream of tears
That have seem to consume the years

For second chances is what life's about
But second loves, without a doubt
To let my heart be free
Let it go, let it be

"Though the love you have may not last forever, know that that person came into your life for a reason. It may not have been what you thought but there was a reason. I have lost love many times and it never feels good, but it always taught me something. The person I thought was the person I would love forever wasn't that person and again that has happened more than once. But the two main people in my life have given me so many things. I will never regret loving them."

"Through love we will receive our greatest gifts and our greatest changes. This is why we must never give up on it."

"It is when I sit in silence that you come to me. All of the emotions and tears flow like rain. So I try not to sit because the silence is to painful."

Living Life.....

"Dream life's biggest dreams...... anyone can dream small."

"I have come to realize that what is important in life is self. Not a vain, conceited, or selfish self, but a loving, caring, mindful person who takes care of themselves so they can give, love and care for others. The one person most often neglected is you and that isn't good for anyone."

"Can you imagine what would happen if we made all the right choices and did all the right things? I know this will never happen, but what if we all tried harder and did better? You have the power to change you and all the things you influence...it's bigger than you think"

"Even in the darkest places beautiful things can grow with a little light. Be the light someone else needs."

"Shine like the brightest star because you never know who is watching you."

"Your actions and thoughts create the world you live in."

"You only have one life to live......how will you choose to live it?"

"Never give up on your dreams.....sometimes they are all we have to keep us going!"

Off in the distance is something waiting for you. Don't let things in life keep you stuck. Take a step in the direction of what you want no matter how small to step.

"Your beauty lies inside of you. No matter what life does to you on the outside, your true beauty will remain. So don't let life steal that too."

"I have had a dream for my life for 3 years now. Working toward that dream and not giving up hasn't been easy. It is a struggle every day, but I believe in that dream. I believe with every part of my being that this dream is meant to be. So every day I just keep going in that direction."

"Have you ever noticed how many times you get upset during the course of your day? The number of times may surprise you. I use to get upset every time I got in the car. People can't drive to save their lives. Then I realized that I wasn't perfect either and sometimes did the very same thing. Once I realized this I didn't get upset much and that was life changing. The more you keep anger and frustration out of your life, the less it comes back in. Have you ever noticed the domino effect once it starts. Stay fully aware of your day and see what happens."

"Do not run through life in fear.....Fear is debilitating."

"Be who you are., not the label that has been put on you. Don't let society form you. Step out of the box."

"Sometimes living life to the fullest has some bumps along the way. Check it like a speed bump and drive on."

"When you believe in yourself your strength multiples 10 fold."

"Why does what other people believe offend you? Everyone has the right to believe what they want. Do you want your right to believe what you want taken away? Condemning others doesn't support your cause at all. All we have to do is love everyone for who they are right where they are. That is all. It isn't for us to say their journey is wrong because we don't know where they are headed."

LOVE FIRST
LOVE ALWAYS

Start Again

Don't let your depression get to you
Don't let it pull you down
Just let your friends be there for you
God has sent them from all around.
You don't have to fight the fight alone
Because that's what friends are for
They probably have been where you've been
So never close the door
Don't let it define you
Or over run your heart
Because it isn't who you are
It's only a tiny part
Fight the fight within yourself
Don't ever let it win
Because each day is new-

                You can just start again

"Bad things come and go, but good things are a state of mind."

"Sometimes life isn't what you think it should be or want it to be. Sometimes life is just life and it goes on even without you. The key is to make the most out of it while you can, with what you have."

"You are dealt a hand that you don't want. Sometimes by your doing and sometimes it is by someone else's doing. Either way it's your hand, play it."

"Why go looking for something you don't really need?"

"If your road is too bumpy, maybe you need to take a new road. It's not the roads fault you are on it."

"Never stop trying to be a better you. Don't let life or someone stop you. The person that will win is you."

"Being able to accept ourselves is one of the hardest things we can do. But in order to have true peace it is a must."

"We think that we have conquered a shortcoming only to find out that it didn't really happen. Sometimes we are being tested repeatedly because we didn't really let go of something we thought we did. Things we struggle with will only go away if we are willing to let go. God will not take something from you if you are just going to take it back."

"Dreams are only dreams until you set out to accomplish them. Take that first step and more steps will follow. Never be afraid to fail, just don't let a step back stop you from taking that next step forward."

"Every journey has an ending. Don't let the ending of one, stop you from beginning another."

"No one person or thing can define you. You define you all by yourself."

"It is often easier to believe in others than it is to believe in ourselves. Why is that, when all you can do is believe in others. You can't make them do anything, they have to do it themselves. So why don't we spend more time believing in the person you can truly change…….yourself?"

"You can only receive great things when your mind and your heart are open."

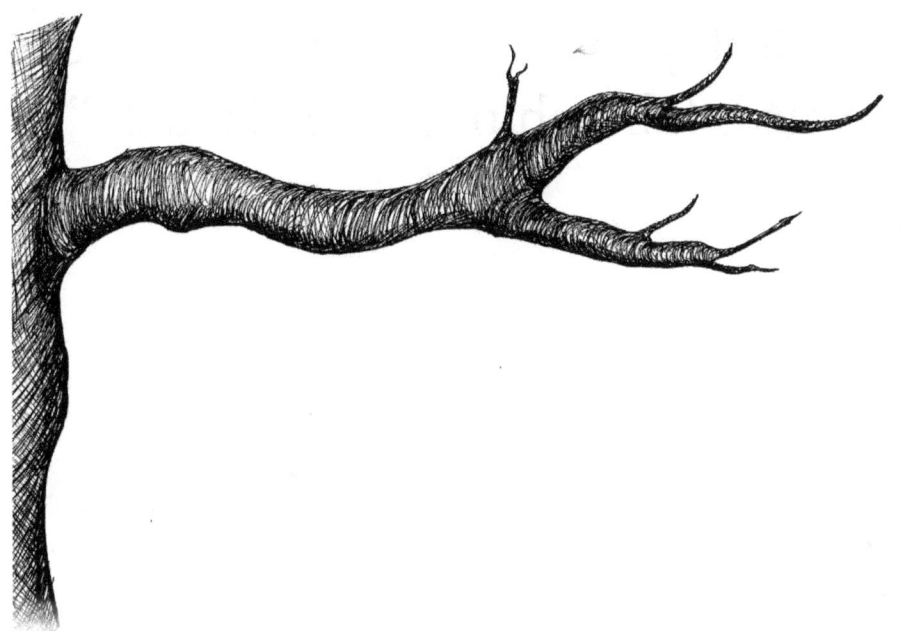

"A lot of days will give you challenges, it's how you process the challenges that will determine how good or bad the day real is."

"Believing in something is half the battle. Your mind is a powerful tool and you can use it to move forward, fall behind, or be struck."

Where The Spirit Leads Us

"If the same negative thing keeps happening to you, you aren't paying attention to the passage or making any adjustments to what you are doing. No one is punishing you. Just trying to show you."

I have learned that it's not about getting what we want. It's about receiving what God gives us. Sometimes what we want is taken away and we don't know why. It's because what we wanted wasn't part of Gods plan. It is hard sometimes to understand the pain we have to go through and just how God's plan fits in. As time passes his plan is revealed. We go on and the pain lessens. It's getting to that point that is sometimes hard to bare and even harder to understand.

"God can bring you out of anything. So, look up. You will not find him on the ground."

"Guided are the paths that we travel, even when we slip."

"Life's journey happens every day. No day passes that doesn't take you somewhere. It may not always be forward. So if you feel you are going backwards, you have to do something to propel yourself forward. Sometimes it's just changing the way you look at things. If you say I can't, you won't."

"I have traveled down roads that I didn't want to travel. I have learned lessons I didn't want to learn. I have come into contact with people I didn't want to meet. And though all of that may seem negative, it all taught me positive things. So really negative things are only negative if you forget the positive that was intended. There is always a message and a reason."

"People are put in our lives for a reason; new friendships, lessons, struggles, growth. They are put there to make us better and push us further. Never take meeting someone new lightly. There is always something for you to come away with, even if it's negative. Any day you can learn something new is a good day."

Lightning strikes
and where it lands
no one knows
it's in his hands
through the storm
the wind and the rain
though somehow it still remains

"Just because you can't see your footprint doesn't mean it's not there."

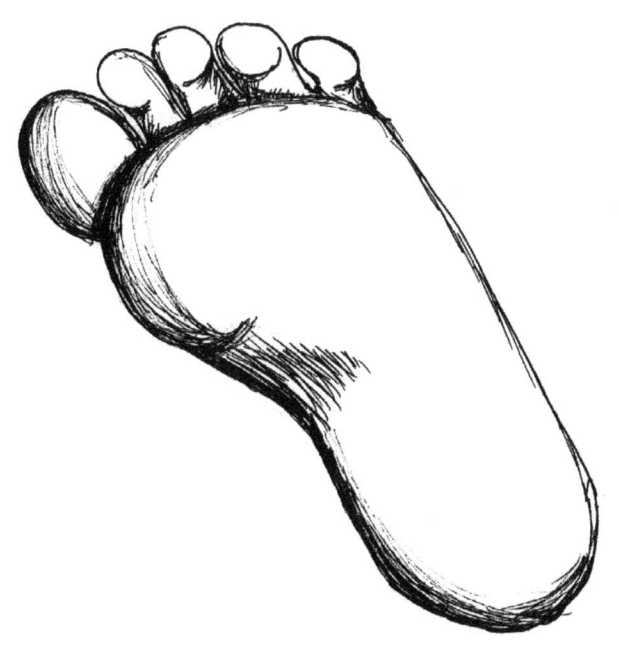

A Single Step

The journeys of life begin with a single step
You'll never have to worry about it being unkempt
For someone watches every step of the way
Knowing you'll make it each and every day
Sometimes you'll fall or stumble
But that will just make you more humble
It will remind you along the way
At the end of the tunnel is the light of day
Looking on the past mistakes
Seeing through all of the fakes
Carrying the torch that one sometimes must bare
But no need to always care
God never leaves us hanging in the night
He's right there beside us in every fight
Knowing we will make mistakes
It is our hand that he takes
His love has been foretold
And never will it unfold

Mr. Turtle

One day I found a turtle
He was so very small
I saw him in the road
And now I recall

How if I would have left him
He probably would be dead
But instead I picked him up
I don't know what was in my head

I just happen to be in a limo
And I put him in the car
It would have been easier
If I'd had a jar

So I set him in a cup holder
Hoping he would stay
But when I looked down
He had gotten away

The first time it happened
I found him in the back
But the next time I looked down
He had fallin in a crack

I began to panic
For he was nowhere in sight
What was I to do now?
But look around with a light

I just couldn't find him
So I got out of the car
Hoping he would come back
And not send me to the bar

My nerves were a little frazzled
Just to say the least
But when I went back
He was there by the seat

The moral to my story
Is one of this-
Never give a ride
To someone off the list

Flickering Lights

Lights flickering in the distance
But change in an instance
As the black of the night passes by
So many of them illuminate the sky

Carrying with them a mystery
The naked eye cannot see
But shining bright never the less
Way up high is where they rest

What lies beyond no eyes can see
  For most of us, it's a mystery

Dreams In The Night

Where do little girls go
When they dream at night
Do they fly like butterflies
Or just hide out of sight

Do they run on the beach
Do they dance on clouds
Do they run barefoot
Or do they sing aloud

Do they dream of the future
Or of faraway lands
Do they dream of a castle
Or just someone to hold their hand

What do little girls dream of
As they sleep at night
It may be a mystery
But I'm sure it's a delight

We all are that little girl
Somewhere deep down inside
And always looking for a prince
That will hold us close at night

We dream of white fences
And lots of pretty things
But all we really want is to be happy
And take what life brings

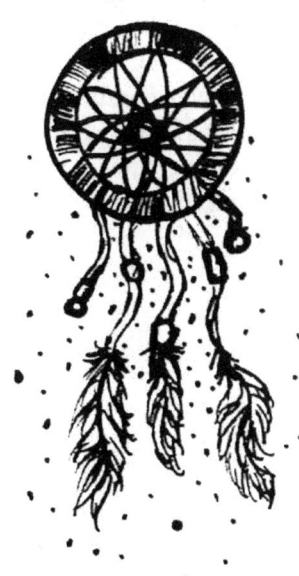

My Spirit Soars

Look into my soul
And what you will see
It's someone so hungry
Just to be free

My heart wants wings
To fly way up high
To see the world
Letting nothing pass by

The beauty that is out there
For all of us to behold
But most never see it
But only in a story that is told

The skies are so bright
The warm breeze that fills
The moon lit night
Then a cool breeze that chills

The forever changing colors
That transforms as we look
But we didn't just read it
It wasn't in a book

Through The Ashes

Sifting through the ashes
To find something you had lost
Isn't always easy
And may come at a cost
But push onward
And keep digging
For its what you must do
For if it's really important
You will find it sifting through
You can't always see things
That are right in front of you
But if you keep digging
It will come to you
Sometimes you have to move things
And look under and around
But if you keep digging
You will be surprise in what you found
Not all things are
The way that they seem
And you will uncover things
That you never dreamed
Some pain and sweat may come to you
But never give up
For if you keep digging
It will be just your luck
To uncover something that will help you
Along the path of life
And open a door
That first cut like a knife

"Why live life by yourself when there is a hand to lead you and a voice to guide you."

"You were perfectly created. Life happens and it has taken you from that, but there are paths that can lead you back. Let go of all the things that life has laid on you. Take only with you the things that have brought you closer to where you are going and let the other things fade away. What has happened to you in life isn't you. What someone else has put you through doesn't define you."

"The body you are in is only a vessel. Who you are is on the inside. So grow that person. Yes we should always take care of the vessel for it is all we have to live in, but what we should look at is on the inside. We tend to care to much about the outside and very little about the inside."

Into The Storm

Do you ever wonder as you drive down the street where the blue lights are going?

Have you ever given thought to the person in the car?

That that person is someone's family member, husband, wife, mother, father, sister or brother?

Did you stop to think why there are laws for the safety of us all?

Well someone lost their blue lights today and someone lost a loved one.

I think about this every time I see emergency vehicle lights, but many don't.

They don't slow down, they don't pull over, it's as if life has gotten in the way of the value of life.

That we are so busy being busy that a couple of seconds would mess up our day.

So remember the next time you see the lights, that it could be someone's life.

It could even be yours or someone you love.

Remember why they turn the lights on in the first place.

And most of all let us remember the ones that have given their lives at the hand of the careless to protect others.

Not Forgotten

A soldier never dies
For his comrades carry him
And they go on with the battle
It might have been your best friend
Or someone you just met
But it doesn't matter
For soldiers are connected
We will always be connected
Only a soldier knows what that means
You can be a thousand miles from home
But if you are with another soldier
You're with family
We can be of all ages
And all walks of life
But all we see is green
So here is to our fallen family
You will never be forgotten
We will continue to carry the torch
In honor of you

Thank you to all of my fellow soldiers past, present and future.

Only a Warrior Knows

As he awakes from a short rest
He is tired
His eyes are blood shot and sore
But he gets up anyway
His body moves slowly
For the scars are many
But he keeps moving anyway
As he goes he knows his purpose
He will do what he does
For few will dare follow
The road he has traveled on
Always fighting for what he believes in
The strength of an army
No matter what comes
Though times has taken a toll
He goes out there anyway
Always focused and with a smile
Life will not take those away
He is driven
But only a warrior knows why
Only a warrior understands
For the mind of a warrior is complicated
It's a feeling you can't really explain
Not just anyone will understand
You have to have been there
To feel
To know
To be

    So he goes out anyway

Great men carve their own destiny. Mediocre men go to work every day at a job they don't like and just exist.

Great men know when and what to do even when things aren't going right. Mediocre men just go with the flow even if it runs them over.

Great men have great people around them, while mediocre men hang out with the same old people they have always hung out with and they are going nowhere.

Great men have great women who support them and lift them up. Mediocre men have women who tear them down.

Great men have been working for a goal all their lives. Mediocre men have no goals.

I have watched many men and women give their lives to the service of this country. People that go unnoticed until something happens. Sometimes good, but mostly bad things that happen. Have you ever gone in a burning building or held someone at gun point or been sent out to cover ground that could have a land mine just waiting for you? Have you had to see a child burned beyond recognition or had to look for body parts of a man hit by a train or hold your buddy who is dying from a bullet wound in your arms? Have you ever been so afraid that it was your day to die, not once, but many times over the years? Most of us will probably never see or feel these things. I would guess that most will never give it a thought. But these are the lives of some every day. Before you point fingers or say harsh words put yourself in their shoes. Did you know that most of these men and women have a hard time being in a loving relationship because of their jobs? Can you imagine how it must feel to be the person that gives so much, yet receives so little? The person that gives all every day for people they don't even know. The level of stress is incomprehensible by most. Police Officers have to go to calls that are a waste of time for stupid things. Firefighters have to go on calls that have nothing to do with fires. Soldiers have to defend things that don't need to be depended. But they have to be ready for the worst at all times. Just imagine what you would do if this were you.

No one asked me to do what I do
I just felt that this is where I am to be
I cannot explain it or describe it to you
I just go to my job and do that I do
Some days are a blessing
Some days are hell
But I wouldn't trade what I do
I wouldn't be you

The intensity of the chase
The guns
The look on his face

Her tears pore down her face
The blood that was left on the stairs
The gun on the floor
The pain of the ambulance pulling away

That day when you save a child from death
The day that your heart can smile
Too bad it can't last for more than awhile

The boots are heavy, much heavier than you think.

Called Into Darkness

As the call goes out, I grab my things and head for the door. We knew this day was coming and had trained hard. This wasn't just any call, but the call. The call that changes history no matter the outcome. But this will change more than history, it will change many lives and lighten many hearts. It will also bring sadness for some. As we load up on the choppers that adrenaline rush kicks in. We sit in silence but yet we all know what the other is thinking. We go over what we trained in our heads. Every move, every door, every step we go over and over in our minds. Then it stops. We all have to clear are heads and relax. In the dark we have to focus. This could be the last time we step out of the chopper. But one by one we step anyway and we wouldn't have it any other way. This is a moment every soldiers waits for. That moment when you can do something for your country that will make a difference. Proud to be a part of one of the biggest moments in history. As we start to move in people start heading our way and we try to make them stop. We continue to move in and start to clear the property one door at a time. Not long after we are there we get the one we are looking for. Shots are fired. We confirm and we take him and all we can carry and move out. We lose a chopper, but get out. The mission is complete and will go down in the history books as one hell of a mission.

ABOUT THE AUTHOR

I few years ago my life changed and I lost everything I had. What I didn't realize at the time that I was about to head in a whole new direction. I combed over my life and processed every inch of it. I was determined to not let anything stop me from what I wanted to do ever again. I wanted to figure out why I was the way I was and why I did the things I did. I had already started on the road to healthier eating and lifestyle, but what was missing was working through the things in my head. We all have things in our heads, but what you do with those things ais the key. As I worked through things I realized with the help of my friends that I was to be a massage therapist. So at 49 I started school. Half way through I decided to go to a health coaching school called the Institute for Integrative Nutrition. I also got my Reiki Master, certificate for the Raindrop Technique and a few other things. All things I didn't even know I wanted to do until I started the first school. I had written the sister book to this one a couple of years earlier, but after starting school I decided I wanted to write a couple more. I have also had some children's books started for years and never finished them. I have accomplished more in the last 3 years than I did in the previous 10 years of my life. I finally know where I'm supposed to be. You have to clear away the cobwebs before you can move forward and now I want more and more. The reason I'm telling you all of this is because I want you to know it's never too late for anything.

Also See "It's the Climb"

Visit me at totalbodyalive.com

www.ingramcontent.com/pod-product-compliance
Lightning Source LLC
Chambersburg PA
CBHW071324040426
42444CB00009B/2080